## Other Titles by the Same Author:

*On the Other Hand: The Little Anthology of Big Questions*

*Just Around the Bend: Más o Menos*

*Louder than a Whisper: Clearer than a Bell*

*Stepping out of Time*

*Umbra, Penumbra & Me* (a compilation of the above four books)

## Children's Picture Books by the Same Author:

*The Frightened Little Flower Bud*    *Ages 4-99*

*Hat*    *Ages 6-99*

*"If you would be a real seeker after truth, it is necessary that at least once in your life you doubt, as far as possible, all things."*

\- René Descartes

The

# DOUBT

FACTOR

For the fluidity of this book, I use the pronoun we a great deal. This is how I see us; we're One. Yes, it's not always appropriate to use the proverbial we, but for the purposes of this book its meaning is general.

# The Doubt Factor

By Renée Paule

Edited by G R Hewitt

Copyright © 2019 Renée Paule

Published in Ireland by RPG Publishing 2019

Cover design and artwork by Renée Paule

All illustrations by Renée Paule

Image 'Society' - Page 71 courtesy of Geralt on Pixabay

Written in British English

ISBN: 978-0-9935098-9-6

For Tommy

No jargon!

*For your convenience there are blank pages*
*for notes at the back of this book.*

# Thank You

Godfrey

# Table of Contents

Preface . . . . . . . . . . . . . . . . . . . . . . . . . . . . . . . . . . . . . . . . . . . . . . . . . . . . . . .*1*

Habits . . . . . . . . . . . . . . . . . . . . . . . . . . . . . . . . . . . . . . . . . . . . . . . . . . . . . .*3*

Escape . . . . . . . . . . . . . . . . . . . . . . . . . . . . . . . . . . . . . . . . . . . . . . . . . . . . .*15*

Next in line . . . . . . . . . . . . . . . . . . . . . . . . . . . . . . . . . . . . . . . . . . . . . . . . .*23*

The Doubt Factor . . . . . . . . . . . . . . . . . . . . . . . . . . . . . . . . . . . . . . . . . . .*31*

Rights and Prejudice . . . . . . . . . . . . . . . . . . . . . . . . . . . . . . . . . . . . . . . .*41*

On Being Bored . . . . . . . . . . . . . . . . . . . . . . . . . . . . . . . . . . . . . . . . . . . .*49*

Food for Thought . . . . . . . . . . . . . . . . . . . . . . . . . . . . . . . . . . . . . . . . . . .*57*

We are One . . . . . . . . . . . . . . . . . . . . . . . . . . . . . . . . . . . . . . . . . . . . . . . . .*65*

Don't Get Me Started! . . . . . . . . . . . . . . . . . . . . . . . . . . . . . . . . . . . . . . .*73*

Authority . . . . . . . . . . . . . . . . . . . . . . . . . . . . . . . . . . . . . . . . . . . . . . . . . . .*81*

Mindset . . . . . . . . . . . . . . . . . . . . . . . . . . . . . . . . . . . . . . . . . . . . . . . . . . . .*91*

Parting Thoughts . . . . . . . . . . . . . . . . . . . . . . . . . . . . . . . . . . . . . . . . . . .*99*

# Preface

It wasn't my intention to write another book about my philosophical journey through life and the quirky traits of humanity, but the many notes and other scraps that found space on my desk thought otherwise and coalesced into the book you now hold. From my perspective, it's been a crazy journey, and still is - a world of confusion and wonder where little makes any sense and that which does, is highly suspect. Some mornings I wake and wonder why there's furniture, a kitchen, books and another 'person' in this place I've learnt to call 'home' - a home that one day I must leave behind forever - along with every one of my 'possessions', friends and family members. None of us has a choice in this matter, for death lurks behind and pursues us relentlessly from the moment we're born - our lives are temporary. This realisation brings a certain tranquillity of mind; things such as my belongings become less important to me, in the sense that I have them, *but* they no longer have me. Each day the fragility of life reveals a little more to me, and whereas I once imagined I was becoming insane, I now know that insanity is leaving me. I could stop my journey at this point, 'retire' and rest on my laurels - just let life happen until I close my eyes for the last time, but I know my restless curiosity won't allow it, and so my life's journey to become 'wise' will continue to its end and whatever lies beyond. Having said that, I'm not so sure I have a choice in the matter at all - though some people might find this state of mind disconcerting, I find it stimulating.

# Habits

*Change always brings about change, and*
*only change will bring about that change.*

Societal conditioning both condemns and encourages our habits; we can't make sense of the contradictions we're surrounded by. One of those greatest contradictions is to self-destruct - ourselves and our planet - and also to take up the initiative to save it all. As we tend to be self-destructive by nature (second nature - therefore a habit) we're going to throw caution to the wind and swing towards the self-destruct side of life. We can for example, spend tens of thousands on saving a neo-natal baby, yet with no thought at all shoot children - indiscriminately - in areas of conflict. Society doesn't make sense and we accept this, provided we're able to make a few complaints here and there! However, compliance (also a habit) will never bring about change.

When I first started writing about habits I imagined it would be fairly straightforward - you know, 'good habits', 'bad habits' and then I'd throw in a few examples of each and discuss the various merits (or demerits) of them, leading to a 'call to action' to change them for the better, or perhaps improve on those that were beneficial in the first place. How wrong I was. The more I looked into the subject of habits the more I became bogged down in the detail - way too complex; notes, notes and more notes all over the place. So I gathered them up - as I've done many times before with other writings - dumped them and started over again - a habit I rather enjoy (the clearing out that is). Below are my findings.

~~~

Habits! Surely these are things that other people have? We don't like to think that we have habits because there's generally a negative connotation to them, but whether we like it or not we're all creatures of habit. If you doubt this, reflect on what you do every day - you'll soon discover that routine and repetitiveness abound; we have many more habits than we care to admit to, even to ourselves. Going back to the 'negative connotation' for a moment, we don't tend to talk about good habits as much as we do the bad (or some would call them conscious and unconscious habits). We have a tendency to notice the negative when it arises; for example, if the cleaners at work didn't clean our workplace properly, we'd notice it straight away and start complaining, but if the place is clean every day we don't even notice their existence - she (or he) gets our attention because something is 'wrong'. How would it feel if you bought your daily paper and noticed that every headline was good news? It might feel disorientating, as we're in the habit of seeing and reacting to bad news - we expect it and accept it with little to no resistance.

Over time, we become so acclimatised to our habits that we don't realise we have them - until, perhaps, someone points them out to us. For example, we may 'umm' and 'err' a lot when we're speaking, have a permanent frown or speak so softly that we can't be heard clearly - our habits become 'second nature', in the same way that putting one foot in front of the other is when we walk. Our habits literally inhabit us and in doing so, become necessary for our continued 'sanity' - much as crutches are to a person with a broken leg. You may be thinking 'so what, that's nothing new and everyone already knows this stuff' and you'd be right. So why do I bother to write about something that everyone already knows? Because, as mentioned in my previous books I'm documenting my life's journey and things I once took for granted, or never took the time to think about, are being brought into sharp focus - that makes them worthy of note and gets me out of the habit of pretending that they don't exist; it's part of the process of that old adage 'know thyself', and know myself I will!

~~~

We tend to associate bad habits with things like nose-picking, an addiction to drugs in their various forms, or the use of foul language and good habits with eating healthily, washing daily and taking regular exercise. Because we look at habits this way, we don't think of them as what they essentially are - necessary for our survival and security. Like all things our habits are best balanced in a way that causes no harm or offence to ourselves or others. Publicly picking our noses, spitting on the pavements or smelling bad shows a lack of self-respect, and a disrespect or contempt for those in close proximity to us - it's not unlike sticking up two fingers at everyone or declaring 'Yeah ... what of it!' By far the habit in all of us that needs changing the most is that of being self-centred, but first we need to recognise - and accept - that we are. I say 'self-centred' in the way we've come to understand it; however, it's impossible for anyone not to be *truly* self-centred, seeing as our world begins with us - being centred in *this* way is an entirely different thing.

Habits are our day-to-day activities - our 'loops', routines and customs - some performed ritualistically on weekdays and others at weekends; some of these habits are essential such as eating, drinking and performing various ablutions. No matter who we are we have habits and to the most extent, perform them unconsciously. Though we're all connected, we each have our unique experiences and memories and these shape what we do or say, the choices we make, and how we habitually feel or react to various circumstances during the course of our lifetimes.

Despite having our unique experiences and memories there's a great deal that we have in common - due to media and authoritative conditioning or if you will 'grooming'. Yes, we *have* been groomed. Groomed to cooperate, to look up to authority despite an abundance of evidence that we shouldn't trust it and to be comforted by our income, families and belongings. We all seek security in one of its many forms - to some that may mean remaining single and to others to have a family of our own, which means looking for Mr or Mrs Right - it may mean seeking a religious leader, an idol to follow or even saving our first million; an illusion of security can be obtained in many guises. Our security is found in the habit of being insecure and seeking security, but as long as we're 'seeking' we'll never find it as it's something that lies within each and every one of us. Having a home of our own and a family to go with it isn't security; after all, we could lose it all at any moment and our lives can become severely disrupted, particularly if we haven't reflected on these possibilities - there's a real danger in forming the habit of taking everything for granted. Real security comes from within and though it can sometimes appear to be 'disturbed', it can never really be disrupted or taken away.

When we observe the larger picture of what's happening all around us, we see that human beings are pretty easy to manipulate provided they're kept occupied - 'usefully' or otherwise. These occupations become new habits; for example, going to work, catching up on soap operas, pubs, sports, reading, climbing, endless crafts, cyber relationships and all sorts of other pastimes. But habits aren't just physical; our thought patterns are habits too. We tend to look at the negative in people (remember the cleaning lady?) During the course of the day most of us will criticise others - if not to their faces, then to someone else or in our thoughts. The negativity mixed with our experiences is rife during the course of our days, and nights for that matter. These thoughts range from a lack of justice in the past, seeking revenge or wanting to make someone 'pay' for what they said or did to us, to things like hatred, jealousy, envy or some other feeling of self-insufficiency. Come on; who amongst us has pure thoughts all day long - most of us couldn't do that even for ten minutes.

Habits can be hard to break - particularly those we have no desire to break, and *that's* what makes the process challenging. When things get difficult most of us give up and carry on doing what we've always done - we draw comfort from familiarity. Realising that this 'second nature' is a part of us goes a long way to knowing ourselves (our habits are the building blocks for what we call our 'character') - our behavioural characteristics. This recognition will inevitably lead to thinking about what our 'first nature' is, which I won't go into here other than to say that we're born curious, desirous, non-judgemental, have an ability to absorb vast quantities of information and are malleable. Habits begin with a trigger; for example, the alarm going off in the morning, the smell of coffee or catching sight of a person we dislike. As a result, we might hit the snooze button, leap out of bed, put the kettle on or go through all the things we dislike about the person we've just seen. What we get out of it all is a certain satisfaction - we get a little more sleep, get to work on time, enjoy that coffee or enjoy perhaps 'getting one over' on the person we don't like in some way. The satisfaction we reap is what tells us to keep the habit going when those triggers are pulled again - It's the reward, and we all enjoy those.

~~~

Habits affect our lives in many ways - we are literally bound by them. We've all lived with other people at some point in our lives - including our families or guardians. Habits can destroy relationships, particularly when we want something done one way and our companion wants it done in another; for example, one person may prefer the dishes cleared up before going to sleep, another when they wake up in the morning. If the one that prefers the dishes washed at night wakes up first and finds the kitchen in a mess (and he can't find a clean coffee cup) conflict will inevitably arise. These conflicts lead to arguments and disorder both in the home and the relationship. Where two or more people live together the home can easily be turned into a war zone when our habits collide. Let's expand this situation to society and its many nations; for example, when one country wants things done their way in another country - we *all* know where this situation leads. Where a person lives alone their habits, as time passes, become so ingrained that it becomes difficult for them to tolerate the presence of another person in their home, and once they leave they'll often feel the urge to return everything to its normal state before they feel comfortable again. I was once married to a man who couldn't wait for visitors to leave - as soon as the front door closed behind them the hoover and cloths came out - erasing any traces of their visit - regardless of the hour.

~~~

Forming new beneficial habits can be hard, but I assure you it's worthwhile and uplifting. We respect and learn to care for ourselves when we do things that are good for us - something that's not possible if we make no effort. A long time ago when I lived in England I took up cycling after having done no strenuous exercise for many years (I was a student) - I became a little overweight. I remember the first time I went out on the bike - it was exhausting, I didn't get very far, and my leg muscles burned from the effort.

The following morning, my muscles ached even more and I struggled to walk; however, I still took the bike out again and managed to get a little further. This pattern went on for 3 weeks and by the end of it I managed several miles. Though my muscles still ached a bit, I felt so much fitter, looked fitter, and was pleased with myself for not having given up. Sometime later I was cycling 12 miles before breakfast every morning and that later led to taking up rowing which I thoroughly enjoyed - I even became a coach. It took a tremendous effort to start cycling and also to remain motivated to carry on, but once I was out every morning I loved every minute of it and consequently, myself too for overcoming the hurdle.

I became ill some seven years ago and this illness meant it was difficult for me to get out and about - I could barely walk 30 metres without gasping for breath; I was in constant pain, had high blood pressure, palpitations, liver disease and couldn't carry shopping or tie my own shoe laces. On top of having to cope with all this I've had hot flushes for the past nine years - around 40-50 a day over a 24 hour period, which has been inconvenient to say the least. Four years after becoming ill and after seeing many doctors, who had no idea what was wrong, and having had many tests and scans, I helped myself with the same determination as when I began cycling. I'll skip the details, but I began walking and built up to a distance of 4 kms most mornings - up and down some pretty steep hills, unless the weather was too bad in which case I used my treadmill; the alternative was to get into the habit of being ill, which I had no intention of doing. I also changed my diet (discussed later in this book). I still get tired, but I'm much better than I was and know that my health is improving a little every day. When we try to change habits, whether by necessity or 'New Year's resolution' it can be disorientating and a bit of a burden - like trying to stop smoking 'cold turkey' or changing from a right-hand drive car to left-hand drive. I've now been driving a left-hand drive car for 14 years and I *still* occasionally go to open the passenger door instead of the driver's. Such a simple matter, but I mention it to demonstrate just how hard it can be - and how long it can take to break some habits, but please don't become disheartened by that.

The more we challenge ourselves the stronger we become and the less afraid we are of difficulty; difficulty is a big obstacle to overcome if we want to change our habits. Habits *are* hard to break and for this reason it's important to replace them with something we enjoy doing that's beneficial to us in some way. Wanting to do things that are good for us is not something we're particularly interested in - would you choose to eat a carrot, or a thick slice of chocolate cake? We eat over-processed foods, junk foods, drink alcohol, stay up late, get little to no exercise and spend an enormous amount of time - sedentary - in front of our various screens; we know that these things are detrimental to our health, yet we keep doing them, regardless. The next obstacle to overcome is not caring properly for ourselves; I'm not talking about regular trips to the hairdressers, dressing nicely or rewarding ourselves for some minor effort we made by going out for a 'slap-up' meal. I'm talking about truly caring - about eating the right foods, cutting out all the snacks and over rich foods and desserts, not smoking or drinking alcohol, taking regular exercise and paying attention to the biggest questions of all 'Who am I?', 'Where did I come from?', 'What am I doing here?' and perhaps also thinking about 'What's next ... and am I adequately prepared for it?'

Here's a challenge for you. Sleep without your mobile phone close by - leave it charging in another room overnight, or at least away from the bed so you won't be tempted to check social media or reply to messages that could wait until morning. The world won't end because your phone isn't close by. If you're resisting the idea then this habit is already deeply 'set', but not unable to be broken - it will be rather difficult, but you're strong enough to do it if you really want to. If the last thing you do at night - or first thing in the morning - is check your messages then this is a worthwhile new habit to adopt. A common resistance to not sleeping with our mobile phones within reach is the possibility of receiving an emergency call and that's a hard one to argue against, but ask yourself how many emergency calls you've ever received - I'm pretty sure you'll still hear your phone ringing in the next room, or out in the hallway. Be alone, be silent, unwind from the day and let these things become a habit when going to sleep at night.

Some habits are essential, like eating and drinking, but we've fallen into some bad ones that are detrimental to our lives and sometimes the lives of others - they do nothing to enhance our lives, becoming burdensome in many ways. For example, a smoker or drinker can be a burden to the whole family or the people they're surrounded by - not just to themselves. However, we're not helpless victims of our habits, unless we choose to be. Habits and traditions structure our lives - they're the anchors that help us to feel safe and secure, but just like a ship that's held fast by its anchor, we'll find it difficult to move away from the situation we've anchored ourselves to and impossible to break free. If we're anchored, we're *not* free and never will be, *until* we make that first move to care more for ourselves *and* those around us. If we don't change the way we live then the world around us - our world - will never change. Observing and changing our thought patterns and physical habits for healthier ones *will* benefit us in the long run - doorways to other paths will inevitably open, if we allow them to. If you want to see a change in the world, you have to be *prepared* to change.

# Escape

*Always end your day a little wiser.*

Escape is something we all do at some point during the course of our lifetime; common ways of doing this are gaming, shopping, new relationships, food and drink excess or going on holiday; there are of course, many more ways to escape and between us, we have them all covered. Look in any holiday brochure and the first word you'll probably see is 'Escape' - to the sun, mountains, seaside or some exotic island. There are many films and books where escape is the theme; the stories are of arduous tunnelling, digging, or some other means to escape from an enemy, prison or some other unpleasant situation that the escapees find themselves in. Is this perhaps how we see our lives - as something to be escaped from? If so what is it we're escaping from, only to come back to? One of the first things we need to do is admit to ourselves that we're constantly escaping from unresolved issues in our lives, and that our escape from them causes us to feel many negative emotions that inevitably result from not tackling those issues; for example, guilt, fear, stress, anxiety and a lack of self-worth; no matter how hard we try, we can't run away from them. Escape can also produce positive emotions like 'satisfaction' from a divertive action we took instead; for example, a long walk or an extra-long session at the gym.

When we escape into our various activities, to some extent we're able to forget about our woes; however, there's an underlying sense of guilt playing on our minds, reminding us of what it is we keep putting off. Gaming for example, could prevent us from getting the haircut we promised ourselves, or from contacting a friend we've neglected for too long. In the case of a neglected friend, whatever our choice of escape, guilt plagues us and we often begin exaggerating to them about how busy we've been, as they fall lower and lower down our priority list. Our minds become overloaded with guilt and excuses and you know what the mind's like - day or night, it won't stop churning. The resulting stress and anxiety become self-perpetuating and the longer it goes on, the harder it will be to break the cycle, and the more we'll need to escape from it. To take the other example, if we put off the haircut long enough then every time we look in the mirror we'll feel negative emotions about the state of the image looking back at us, reminding us that gaming is more important than anything else - more important than ourselves, or our friends and family; our empty words can't make it up to them. Other things we try to escape from are looking for a job, seeing a doctor, cleaning our homes - whatever our form of escape we're only putting off the day we must eventually face up to the issues we avoid. Stress, anxiety and a lack of self-worth become the norm, which is an unhealthy state of affairs for ourselves or anyone in close proximity. Whatever we do to escape, like watching films or playing games or taking a holiday, when it's over we're back in the real world, which once again, drives us straight back into escape mode.

We escape into our 'worlds' because it's fun and easy to live in them, provided we don't mind feeling the stress or anxiety *and* provided we can live with a lack of self-worth - a small price to pay considering the effort needed to face up to ourselves; it's never easy, but when we make that effort, it pays dividends and once we see this we become much nicer people to be around; we even enjoy our *own* company more. If we don't change then surely our lives are being lived for no good purpose as we go through the motions in the space between birth and death, lazily drifting into our graves. As mentioned in the previous chapter, after I began cycling, my life became richer and I liked myself much more - *because* I made the effort. The alternative was to do nothing to improve my health and fitness and resign myself to being unhappy with my life. The results of the effort I made meant that I was better equipped to tackle other problems that arose in my life without needing to escape from them; when we win one battle, we become emboldened to face others. Tackling the things I avoided strengthened my resolve and though it took several more years, I was able to do what I'd been putting off for so long - to write with purpose, and that led to the production of my first book.

Our lives should be fun and easy, but we don't live in that kind of society; we live in a society that escapes from what's real - let's face it, it *is* a bit of a mess - into a fantasy world, which is well structured and - to a large extent - leaves us expecting happy endings. What we actually do is surf on and absorb fantastic amounts of information and just like with the sea, one wave leads to another. An example of this can be found on websites like YouTube, or its brothers and sisters; who doesn't visit them at some point to watch videos? When one video is finished there are many recommendations as to what to watch next and most of us click on them. We may begin by watching a music video and end up hours later watching a documentary about planetary destruction, and so on and so forth - it's not unlike Chinese whispers. The 'wormhole' we dove into is never ending and as much as there's good information in some of these videos, there are far more that society would be better off without. We don't just dive into these wormholes, we are deliberately drawn into them. 'Why', doesn't matter - what matters is realising that this *is* happening. While doing just that, I came across this excerpt that amused me.

> *A wormhole is a theoretical passage through space-time that could create shortcuts for long journeys across the universe … [b]ut be wary: wormholes bring with them the dangers of sudden collapse, high radiation and dangerous contact with exotic matter.*
> *https://www.space.com/20881-wormholes.html*

The more time we spend in these 'wormholes', fantasy worlds, either through games, videos, films or books, the more we struggle to see or cope with what's 'real'.

We love adventure stories, mysteries, dramas, fantasy adventures, comics, romance novels, science fiction, games, crime and so much more. Comfort can be found in alcohol, drugs, celebrations, sports and a whole host of other things to suit every taste. Along with the above, every media headline drives us further into our fantasies and though there's nothing really wrong with that, they won't raise our consciousness level or make us *really* happy. These occupations help us to forget about the difficulties we face in the world.

My own way of escaping was to move house frequently - I used to love moving and settling into a new home and/or relationship and as soon as I was settled, I'd tend to move again. I was moving from monotony, comfort, boredom or anything familiar - anything that led me to a place where I had to change and had the time to do it. I always wanted something new, but now I know that each move wasn't new at all - it was more of the same in a different house, with a different face to look at. I wasn't changing - I was escaping!

We all like to escape from something in our lives. We're trying to find 'happiness' in an unhealthy environment - a world that isn't happy at all, and it's quite a challenge. We look for validation, gratification or perhaps just pleasure - any way of confirming or at least acknowledging that we exist or that we can do something well. We escape into illusion and in this illusion we find refuge - it becomes a place of safety. We live in a disordered chaotic world that can be uncomfortable at times. Consequently, we seek the most beautiful thing that we can have in this existence - love. Our dreams are full of the quest for love and with that love, we hope to find acceptance of who we are and all that we wish to become in our lives - to be in an unconditional relationship. We seek this love from wherever we can get it and I'm *not* talking just about 'romantic' relationships; we seek to be loved and appreciated by anyone who'll take a second glance at us - a glance in which we can show them what lies behind the masks we wear, without fear of criticism, threat or attack of any kind. We'd love to make ourselves vulnerable, but society doesn't allow us to do that - we have to be tough, stoic and societally stable - to give the impression that we're 'together', when really none of us are. We need to feel appreciated and worthwhile and as most of us don't, we seek to escape from the stresses, worries and problems that arise from being separated from love. Yes, we have been separated from it - why else would we be looking for it? A child that's lost sight of a parent in a shopping centre for example, will be unhappy until it's reunited with them again; we all suffer from this condition - we've been separated from our root - and we commonly call the symptom that results from that separation, loneliness.

When we spend our time doing things that merely 'occupy' or divert us, we can't discover what it's like to experience inner-happiness or to know what it feels like to overcome the difficulties that drive us to 'escape' from what's really going on, by doing something that's *good* for us. When I used to go cycling early every morning I felt amazing *because* I'd made the effort to do something positive for myself, and that feeling lasted all day. Now I get that same feeling when I walk my 4 kilometres each morning - sometimes while it's still dark and sometimes a little later. There are days when a voice in my head says 'you don't have to bother today' and it can be tough not to listen to it, especially if it's cold or raining. I've learnt to ignore it, because I get a buzz after my walk and that's a much nicer feeling than the feeling I'd get if I didn't go. Getting through the rest of the day *knowing* that I've had my exercise makes me feel *good* - there's no guilt nagging at me because I didn't make the effort. We have to get on with the things we keep putting off (now, not later) and *then* we can feel that gratification and acknowledgement that we long for - it comes from within and not from someone or something else. We *never* feel good when we don't take care of ourselves, but rather we suffer, feel anxious and guilty all day about not doing the things that benefit us. There's a voice that has our best interest at heart, and one that doesn't - which one we choose to listen to is up to us.

# Next in line

*A seed is planted, grows, produces
more seeds, and then dies.*

Whether we like it or not the human experience is not unlike that of a seed. We're born, we grow, we have children, and then - sooner or later - we die. Some of us don't get to complete the cycle in much the same way as some seeds don't germinate or some flowers die sooner than others, perhaps never having produced any seeds of their own; this is the nature of nature - it is a whole - no one seed is more important than another. The seeds of our world are plentiful and nature has ingenious ways of assuring that its innumerable varieties of seeds are continuously produced in order to ensure its survival. It's the same with mankind; the continuance of mankind is assured all the while male and female are attracted to each other and nature takes its course - this is unlikely to change in any significant way. However, if mankind continues to abuse itself and the world in which it must live, in the way that it does, the quality of life in our future - both in nature and for the vast majority of humankind - is looking unnecessarily and increasingly bleak. In our arrogance, we tend to forget that nature doesn't need us to survive, but we *do* need nature to nourish and sustain us. I don't wish to get into the science of these things; the point is that nature, in any of its forms, has the advantage of numbers thus assuring that our world continues; there's always a 'next in line' - perhaps altered unfavourably in some way, or perhaps not. This is an important fact to grasp if we're ever to come to terms with so many 'awkward' truths about how we live in our world.

This 'next in line' pattern has been copied - by us - many times over. Here are several examples of that:

- A new fashion doesn't last very long; its successor suffers the same fate - often borrowing from some previous fashion.
- If a soldier is killed or injured, another will quickly take his place.
- Mistakes and heartaches - we all know about these.
- Disasters - follows the same pattern; think about newspaper headlines. We have many disasters occurring concurrently.
- There's always someone waiting to fill our position at work - no matter how indispensable we believe ourselves to be.

- Next in line for retirement!
- Birth and death! Yes, I know we don't like to think about the latter, but it's as true as birth.
- We replace a worn-out pair of shoes with a new pair.
- This book is also a 'next in line'.
- The next 'guru' we follow perhaps?
- The next meal, day, night, friend.

I could go on and on with this list, but reflecting on the concept of 'next in line' is something we could all benefit from. Of course, finding the time to do this is not easy with our busy schedules and the many distractions calling on that time, but it *is* worth taking a few moments out of our day to ponder these things. Life and everything we do or produce in it, is temporary and self-perpetuating. We live in a society that encourages the replacement of just about everything (and everyone), and there's more of this to come in the not-so-distant future - we've not yet wisened to this fact or the fact that we're not - in the least bit - encouraged to think about subjects such as these; quite the contrary, we're given many distractions to divert our attention *away* from intelligent thought. The things we're distracted by are the things that hold us back from change, from personal growth, from raising our consciousness level and from realising that this is not 'it'. We can't realise this until we look at the structure of our lives. We live in a reality where things wear out, including ourselves; as the old adage says, 'ashes to ashes' - it's our physical nature, but it's *not* our end.

When we leave a job, home or even a relationship, someone is always waiting in the side-lines - ready, willing and able to take our place - not in the same way perhaps, (we each have something unique to offer every situation) and not always immediately. Everything happens in its own time, when we're ready for it and not a moment before. In the same way, when we change our lives even slightly, it follows that our life will head off in a different direction - it *must*. In my experience, this has usually been for the better and though I've made mistakes again and again - and paid for them - I've always reflected on them enough to make me into a stronger and (I like to think) more centred person. I was once impulsive in all walks of my life, but these days I reflect before making any decisions and consequently, make fewer mistakes.

~~~

Given all of the above, is it any wonder that we strive to 'succeed' within the confines of the society we created - a society that's narrow-minded and *so* physically orientated that it strives to hold onto that which must die. When we look at the situation from a distance it has the effect of rendering each one of us superfluous to the agenda or needs of society - each of us is easily replaced, as though we were toys to be discarded. There are so many of us that are unneeded, unwanted and unnoticed, and this leads to a general feeling of unworthiness and loneliness, particularly if we disagree with the way society is evolving. Our society only has room for those who are willing to comply with it - a compliance that offers no resistance whatsoever - ironically, making us the slaves of the very system we've created. This kind of society creates places *within* it for those who look for nothing *outside* it and we are so many, that the competition for places is fierce. We are of course each one of us a part of that society, but the *majority* shape it and resist any change. The majority of us are wasting our lives and under the illusion that we are in some way, making the most of a bad situation. Others seek change and learn that they can't change the majority mindset and *that's* when the realisation dawns that we're only able to change ourselves.

In a society such as this we create depression, anxiety, fear, disease and sorrow - this low vibrational living can't sustain us in any beneficial way. How *can* it when it doesn't work for the benefit of each one of us, but instead creates both wealth and poverty, sickness and health, truth and lies, and order and disorder - a world where nobody *really* cares about anybody else, unless it's expedient to do so. Nobody really knows whether they're coming or going - there's nothing we can truly believe in or make sense of. We are each so easily replaced, just like last year's mobile phone, other gadget or worn-out appliance and it's for this reason that we hold on so tightly to our relationships and possessions - they provide the illusion of stability and permanence and for some, that illusion is a comfortable nest to reside in; it's a safe haven for living out our lives, until whatever's 'next in line' arrives - our so-called death.

In a world such as ours, having something 'next in line' is inevitable. We're born and we must *all* die, so it follows that in order for this world to continue, someone must one day take our place, just like we have taken the places of those who were here before us. There's little value in a population that lives the way we do; we live for what we can get out of this world - or inherit from it - while we're still alive, rather than for what we can give to and leave with it, to make it a better place to live - a place our children can inherit and live peacefully in.

So why is it important to think about 'next in line'? It's important because while we're living in our comfortable 'nests' we don't think about what's 'next in line' *after* this life. Existence and evolution will roll on without us - regardless - but I'd suggest that our mindset remains with our *Self*. I'd also suggest that each one of us is here to grow, to raise ourselves to a higher level of consciousness, despite the lack of encouragement or motivation to do so. When we take a look at the state of humanity, not just today, but how it's *always* been, 'why' becomes obvious. I'd suggest that our death is something it would be wise to prepare for, and further, that death doesn't arrive and make everything 'alright'. I don't subscribe to beliefs that after death we'll find ourselves laughing our heads off - with our deceased loved ones - about the horrible 'game of life' we all created, in which so much suffering and sorrow took place, or that we'll be amused at how afraid we were of that world. When we go to a party, we dress up for it. When we go shopping, we make sure we have the means to pay for it. We fill our car with fuel before embarking on a journey. We prepare ourselves for *absolutely* everything, but not our death, and unlike everything else, we've no idea when that will occur *or* what's 'next in line' for us, which for me is a sobering thought worth considering.

# The Doubt Factor

*To doubt is to question, and to question*
*is a part of our quest; our quest is to find*
*our truth and through it, to grow.*

Doubt is a powerful and underestimated word whose meaning can safeguard or vanquish. We don't tend to be aware of its significance in our lives, or just how complicated we've made it. We plant, manipulate and use it to form and sway opinions, but it only throws us into a quandary; 'Does God exist?', 'Is someone guilty or not?' Doubt creates fear, dread, anger, judgement, suspicion, limitation and above all, uncertainty; when we feed our doubts we give them power over us, and over our opinions of others too. Doubt can make a lie true and truth a lie, or more often it can leave us with a debilitating sense of insecurity between the two - it creates the so-called 'grey area' that has far too many shades. However, where there's a lie, there must exist a truth that it's masking - such is the nature of duality. Doubt has no conclusion and doubt leads to the greatest form of procrastination - being unprepared for 'what's next', if anything at all.

Doubt is a seed planted into the fertile soil of the mind by, amongst other things, insecurity, the media, gossip, jealousy and mischief - doubt requires no proof whatsoever. Once planted, how it grows is up to the individual - it can either be rooted out, or nurtured and allowed to flourish, bearing deadly fruit whose seeds can then be re-planted into the impressionable minds of others. Doubt causes a lot of harm; for example, to innocent people whose reputation has been called into question. Often, regardless of any evidence to the contrary, we tend to believe the 'plant', ignoring other possibilities for its existence, such as malicious intent. Even if we don't believe what's been said about a person, the mention of their name causes us to remember what we were told and, perhaps wonder if it could possibly be true; doubt is like a barbed hook that can't easily be removed without leaving a scar - how many times have we heard that old adage 'Ahh, but remember, there's no smoke without fire'; how we *love* to doubt. We know very well how this information is distributed in the media and social circles, yet too often we're willing to judge someone based on what another has said about them. Those who plant this sort of doubt don't have good intentions towards the person (or persons) they're demeaning, but are serving their own agenda. If enough attention is given to a 'plant' the public's head is easily turned against the victim or in the case of friends, one pitted against the other. Of course sometimes the 'plant' may be *true*, and this is how we often end up not knowing what to believe or what not to. The long term effect can make us suspicious of everyone and everything - not a healthy state of mind for society to be in.

We need to learn to doubt intelligently and above all, of our own volition. We're blinded by too much misleading and unwise information - information born from fear - put in place by those who are happy for the majority not to reflect on philosophical or spiritual matters, because they themselves are afraid. For this reason they keep the population under tight control and we allow them to do it. Who are the people who have done this? We are; we've put our *own* obstacles in our way - first and foremost of these are the authorities that we allow to rule over us; these are the people who thrive on the energy of others. There *is* of course information that encourages us to ponder these things, but the majority of people aren't ready or currently able to consider it - it requires a different way of thinking that evolves through pretensionless self-reflection, and an ability to doubt *everything* we've ever been told, by others, and as feedback from our senses; unfortunately, we tend to have too much on our minds to cope with anything new and uncertain. Our education on these subjects is non-existent; we learn about everything *outside* of ourselves, but never *about* ourselves. It doesn't matter where we look in the world for truth; for example, in libraries, museums or the media - we can only find it by going within and - to reiterate - *only* by going within. This process has been so severely deprecated that few are prepared to begin their journey, mostly because 'within' each one of us are too many horrors to face - horrors we've learnt to skilfully conceal from ourselves, and also from others. Deep down we know this, which is one of the reasons why we avoid it - we have an innate need for self-protection. If something has been hidden, it follows that *someone* must have hidden it; if something has been hidden, it also follows that it can be found, albeit not easily. If we're not our own masters, we both need and invite protection from others, and there's no shortage of people willing and able to offer it to us.

Who first decided that a mirror is an accurate portrayal of what we look like and why does it need to be perfectly flat? I'd suggest that this idea came from water; have you ever looked at a perfectly still lake and seen the reflection in it? I've looked at my face in a still lake, but I'm still not sure that the reflection is what I truly look like - a breath of wind distorts the whole image; a slight bend in a mirror distorts our image too. Have you ever looked at yourself in a 'hall of mirrors'? When I look at the moon with my glasses on I see one image, and a different one when I take them off again. After much reflection on these matters I find myself doubting the validity of everything I set my eyes upon, and consequently my own existence - I can't be certain of anything at all, whether I'm wearing my glasses or not.

Life isn't interesting when we think we know everything - it becomes interesting when we understand that we don't. Adventure is a trip into the unknown - of uncertain outcome - not to somewhere familiar; it's the uncertainty that makes it exciting, and uncertainty that arouses our curiosity. The greatest excitement in receiving a wrapped package comes from *not* knowing what's inside - from the journey of expectancy that leads to the surprise; it's the adventure. This sense of adventure is always seen in very young children - they don't see dangers because they don't know danger, which is why we protect them from it. A child will run into the road without looking to see if a car is coming - there's no doubt in their mind that they can reach whatever it is they were attracted to. If we were to shout 'STOP' while they were in the middle of the road they would become confused - be in doubt about the command - and therein lies another danger, as they may freeze in front of an oncoming car. When we teach children danger - doubt creeps in - and with that doubt they lose their sense of adventure, curiosity and their creativity; they gradually learn how to navigate safely through their increasingly dangerous world. *Of course* we have to teach children to be safe - we've created a society with danger just about everywhere we turn, and it's our responsibility to protect them from it. As a result of this, when we're grown up, we tend to enclose ourselves behind walls and doors (in offices or homes) - in many ways, we create an environment where *we* are the contents of the 'wrapped package', and our doubts about a brighter future keep us there. The point is, when we doubt we can do something, we can no longer do it - we become afraid as more and more dangers are put on our paths. If we're afraid, we look for a place of comfort and security - both mentally and physically - and in that place there's no adventure, peace of mind or growth - there are only conformity and dependency.

~~~

The mind loves certainty, so when we have to make a choice and hit that 'doubt moment' certainty evaporates into thin air - we become unclear not only of what we *think* we want, but in what we choose in its place. Doubt is the 'Umm' and the 'Ahh' part of decision making. Where there's choice, there's conflict - a 'not knowing' which choice to make; think of it this way - if we *knew* what we wanted, there would *be* no choices. Doubt feeds on the fear of imagined consequences, such as making a mistake we may later regret; doubt holds us in a state of indecision as our mind writes and re-writes possible conclusions - it becomes our master. In the end, weary from the mental gymnastics, we shut our eyes and take the first bottle our hand touches - 'Oh why do there have to be *50* varieties of salad dressing?' Doubt runs through the complete spectrum of our lives - from choosing a simple condiment to the feeling we may get when walking 'down the aisle' - the uncertainty that we're doing the 'right' thing; I've done this enough times to know what I'm talking about. Doubt both leads and misleads us and how this manifests in our individual lives depends on our individual experiences, beliefs and backgrounds; for example, one person may wish to go to university but deep down, doubt their ability to thrive in such a demanding environment; someone from another background may have doubts about their faith. In both cases, doubt causes mental and physical stress with its attendant consequences - what we *really* doubt - whatever the circumstances, is ourselves. If we aren't clear in our thinking, doubt will shake and break our very foundations - if we allow it to - and we all know what happens to a house when the foundations become unstable. For this reason the majority of us are happy to accept our 'lot', as we don't have to make any life-changing decisions - our foundations, however unstable, remain shored up.

~~~

Truth in society is just about impossible to find, yet still we keep searching for it, knowing that it can't be found. Take religion for example - what an angry mess we've made of this wonderful word and all it should stand for. Scientists look up through telescopes or down through microscopes at our universe and, despite their best efforts to dissect what they see, they only really see 'wonder', and create theories about that wonder. If we would only look at the world with 'wonder' and stop *there*, instead of dismissing it as some sort of convenient cosmic accident. Wonder can't be analysed, taken apart or split - it can't be doubted or demolished either - wonder *is*, and we're a part of it. Life is out there waiting for us to discover, believe, ponder over, or to ignore. Can you in all honesty believe that our lives are so insignificant - that we were born to live fly-by-night existences that have no value? That our place in the universe doesn't warrant, at the very least, our personal curiosity? We live in doubt - doubting a lie or a truth and not knowing whether to turn left or right for fear of error or judgement; we deny the obvious, even when it's crystal clear.

There's no space, between the left and right, between the lie and truth or between black and white, but the finger of doubt has smeared a 'line' producing a grey area of uncertainty where things can be a little bit true, or a little bit false, if not a 'little bit pregnant' too; it's the haystack that hides the needle - the dark cloud that engulfs us; it's the mass of uncertain information that we're slowly drowning in. To make sense of our world we need to *stop* trying to make sense of it - to turn off the noise and give ourselves space to think about the predicament we're all in. By pulling back - even a little - we begin to get clarity, a clarity that grows as we develop a greater understanding of our fears, dread, anger, judgement, suspicion and limitations - they diminish as we pull further and further away from the confusion, into a space where there's just silence and wonder - a space where we can grow. We may not believe that this is possible, because we haven't been taught to think in this way, but surely it's wiser to opt to live in a space that gives us the opportunity to be deeply and truly content, as opposed to a place that leaves us bewildered and alone? In the world of chaos, sometimes it's more restful for us to give 'wonder' the benefit of the doubt.

# Rights and Prejudice

*To get rid of prejudice in society we have
to change hearts - not the law.*

We live in a world where 'rights' have transcended to an almost godlike status and can be called upon in practically any given situation as authority to justify our actions. We have 'individual' and 'group' rights and in many cases the rights of the group override those of individuals; for example, a baker may, for one reason or another, object to putting a particular symbol on a celebratory cake he's been asked to create; his customer however, calls him prejudiced and demands his legal right not to be discriminated against - the baker's rights are abrogated. In an attempt to 'legislate out' prejudice in society we have created an unworkable system of laws that fuel prejudice rather than remove it. Ironically, the 'rights' that grant us so much 'freedom', have become more like shackles, in that it becomes almost impossible to object to anyone or anything, without treading on some right or another. We tend to agree with what we've been told - and if we're honest - keep our prejudices firmly locked away for fear of being 'politically incorrect' - we keep silent about them and not to do so is tantamount to creating a 'breach of the peace'. Our prejudices however, are not so easily disposed of - they're deep rooted in our social *and* inherited conditioning. The 'powers that be' consist of human beings, just like us, and are therefore also prejudiced - we're uncertain how to correct this over-complicated situation; regardless, a great many of us are perfectly happy with things the way they are, provided we're not directly affected by them. Consequently, we live in a state of uninterrupted turmoil with no apparent resolution in sight - us *versus* them, as it's always been.

What are rights? If they belong to any one of us, then they belong to *each* and *every* one of us - no one human being has the right to cause the suffering of another. To cause the suffering of another human being is a terrible thing that reduces us to a state of barbarian, and we *do* cause the suffering of others - sometimes deliberately and sometimes inadvertently - to such a large extent that I often feel ashamed to be a member of the human race. To spend small fortunes on for example, going into outer space, when we haven't ensured the right of every human being to have adequate food, water and shelter saddens me beyond the realms of grief. If we can't live intelligently on our own planet, what atrocities are we destined to commit on others? We speak of ourselves as 'advancing' but when we look at this objectively, it couldn't be further from the truth - technology is advancing, yes sure, but humanity is in rapid decline; what's the good of the one without the other, and to whom? As if this message isn't strong enough we now live in a world of so-called 'entitlement' - believing we're deserving of the rights we demand; the right to be protected and supported by the system that's destroying us - a system that paradoxically, we protect and support. At this point, I haven't the heart to go any further into this subject - you know this stuff as well as I do - so let's move on.

~~~

What is prejudice? It's pre-judgement - judgement, without knowledge or evidence; prejudice is a conditioned response to anything at all - favourable or not. We're taught when we're very young that a colour - for example - is blue, and we believe it for the rest of our lives - we accept this information at face value, as we have no prior knowledge, evidence or reason to question it any further. In no time at all we know 'blue' in all its shades; blue is for boys, blue means sad, blue is the colour of our sky, the sea, and blue is cold - woe betide *anyone* who tells us otherwise. At the other end of the colour spectrum we have red and all its shades; red is for danger, anger, it's sexy, hot and the colour of a lovely sunset. Information and all its symbolism are ingrained in us and so are our judgements of them; for example, women are this, men are that, the French do this and the British do that - there's no need for me to be specific here. We can't look at anything without judging it in some way; we've opinions and pre-judgements about absolutely everything - some of these are belligerent and antagonistic; we've been conditioned and manipulated to be this way by our families, the media (particularly comedy), our teachers and various *agents provocateurs*. *All* prejudice has a beginning. Any form of prejudice limits our ability to be objective, as *none* of it is born from intelligent thought, but rather by the menacing and mischievous action of tradition. Prejudice causes distress and suffering in others, as well as ourselves. No-one likes to be judged or categorised by anyone else - it's bullying at *any* level and in any situation.

It's clear to me that we once lived together without borders or barriers - although in our known history we didn't live together in peace, or without prejudice. The mindset that created these borders had no good intentions, and still doesn't. Imagine one piece of land, and then divide it and give each piece a different name, create different cultures on each of them, sell off portions of the land and then set one owner against another. This action - which we have taken for many thousands of years - is immature and mischievous, and we haven't had enough of it yet - we create new borders all the time and this action further separates us from each other. The barriers are not only physical - they manifest themselves in race, wealth, status, gender and class, to name but a few. We're so far apart from each other that the task of coming together again seems to be impossible, particularly when given the short duration of our lifetimes; how can we hope to change things that have been going on for so long, perhaps for millions of years? It's a nonsense to remain in this state and though we can't - as individuals - bring us all together again, we can strive to remove our *own* borders and barriers by seeing the ridiculousness of the situation - intelligent thinking *grows* in us when we're willing to embrace it.

Prejudice forces us into groups of various kinds; nations, families, companies, committees, schools or religious groups - prejudice causes separation and favouritism. We become proud of our nations for example, and consequently have differing opinions of others; some of us may reject our nation and wish to be resident elsewhere, and some of us are so ashamed of our place of birth that we claim to be a different nationality altogether, usually due to prejudice of one kind or another - we become prejudiced against ourselves. Although it was never the case in my experience, families tend to 'stick together' before lending a hand elsewhere; you know the expressions as well as I do - 'blood is thicker than water', 'family first', 'all in the family', etc. One problem with these groups is that if you dare to think differently from them, you no longer fit in and in many cases, are no longer welcome - conflict arises. We suffer from loneliness and the thought of being excluded from our 'group' can lead us to remain compliant within it, become the so-called 'black sheep' or less often, to leave; we generally, however, have nowhere else to go so the latter option is not always viable. Ironically, groups - although they imply solidarity - actually separate us from each other.

If we're ever going to be free of prejudice in our lives, it's important to understand how we became prejudiced in the first place and in most cases, this was by our births into a particular cultural group, or groups. From day one we began to be conditioned by our parents, who in turn had been conditioned by *theirs* and so on down the line. We didn't arrive at the conclusions or prejudices we have by our own investigations, but rather we accepted them on trust without the ability to validate their authenticity - we were too young and powerless to make valued judgements, or if we did make them, they were dismissed as inconsequential chatter. As time progressed, these prejudices were reinforced by peers, anecdotes, cultural norms and the various media *et al* and we would hold them 'dearly' without really knowing why - often enjoying the camaraderie from, for instance, hurling abuse (verbal or otherwise) at the targets of our prejudices and ironically, knowing nothing about them other than the fact that, for some unknown reason, we didn't like them. There's no intelligence in this type of behaviour - there's no intelligence in *any* conditioned behaviour. Are we a hopeless case, doomed to perpetuate our prejudices and pass them on to others or is there something we can do to halt the process? How about the next time we feel our prejudices arising we take a moment to look at them and see what's really happening to us? We need to learn to look at the structure of society 'now' and to decide what part we wish to play in it - go with the flow, or break ranks and begin to think for ourselves. We could, for example, observe our own prejudices by observing our reactions to any given situation; for example, what prejudice arises when we walk down the street, when we listen to the news, when we're at work, or when we're trying to get to sleep at night. Who do we like, who do we hate and who are we indifferent to - and why do we feel this way - do we have reasons rather than just reactions? The noise in our minds will be greatly reduced if we pay attention to these things - with the correct intention, which is not for any personal gratification, but rather for personal growth. We have to drop our prejudices if we're going to change our world. To get rid of prejudice in society we have to change our hearts - *not* the law. Our task here is to surpass whatever may be thrown in front of us - no matter how horrible; we have to grow out of our circumstances and our prejudices, before we can become 'whole' again.

# On Being Bored

*Being bored is a wonderful thing - if only we'd take a moment to make friends with it.*

When we're bored time slows to a crawl - we look at the clock after what seems like an hour and only minutes have passed. We may check to see if the clock is still working properly; we've all experienced this phenomenon at some time or another. Why does time pass so slowly? Perhaps it's the same effect we feel when driving off a motorway and we suddenly have to slow down - it feels an eternity at 30 mph after our galloping 70 (or more). Our brains are forced to put the brakes on, but our minds are still racing ahead - they don't want to slow down because we have things to do, places to go and people to see. On another occasion we may be bored because we're waiting for something or someone, and sometimes because we have nothing to wait for and nothing to do. Yet there's a great irony; when we're bored, really *really* bored, nothing seems to interest us and suggestions to alleviate that boredom are too frequently rejected as 'boring'. Why are we bored? The honest answer to this is that we're not doing the things that best suit human beings - ironically, being bored, being quiet, just *being*. We seek stimulation elsewhere, somewhere more exciting and livelier, of which there's a surfeit of opportunities. We also seek it by being busy and bored; for example, at work, which for the majority of us is uninspiring and monotonous, which is why we look forward to our weekends and holidays so much - for most of us, work is a thankless task. We don't know how to be by ourselves, doing nothing, because we're in a constant state of busyness - flitting from one thing to another, but rarely as 'authentic' human beings - unhindered by *artificial* intelligence. We do what we're conditioned to do and seldom anything else, without being labelled a rebel that is.

We're taught to be busy in our childhoods; the majority of us are ceaselessly occupied and stimulated (too often *over*-stimulated) during our waking hours - by our surroundings, observations, siblings, parents, friends, educators, entertainers and our books, toys, puzzles etc. - almost as if it were an 'offence' to do nothing. These days *additional* stimulation comes from our electronic devices too; I've witnessed very young babies reaching for the devices of their parents - somehow, they're irresistibly attracted to them. It's only a matter of time until children discover the vastness of the internet on their own devices - too short a time; once on their screens, it's near on impossible to divert their attention away from them without temperamental consequences; there's always a new video to watch, something to 'like', someone to follow, to unfollow, or a new inspirational quote to share - leaving us anything but inspired. Whatever our circumstances, there's always *something* to occupy us - boring or otherwise; even when going to a local park we're occupied with swings, slides and roundabouts. The opportunity, or encouragement, to be 'silent', still, or to reflect on our very existence doesn't arise; it wouldn't enter the mind of most parents to think about this themselves, let alone encourage their children to do so. If parents need peace and quiet to get on with what they're doing, it's far too easy to place children in front of a television, or computer, at which point proxy-parenting takes over. From a very young age our minds are overloaded by external sources - so much so that we don't know how to be 'silent'; silence has become an uncomfortable and frightening place to be - to be avoided - as we were never introduced to, encouraged to appreciate, or to think about the wonder of it.

Acclimatised to noise and chaos, and as past occupations no longer stimulate our children, they become bored and that boredom leaves them desperately seeking stimulation elsewhere. They may scream and shout, not really knowing why they're unhappy (a tantrum) or they may mope about, break their toys, annoy those around them and generally make a nuisance of themselves. But, what's really happening is that they're struggling with boredom and the lack of any new stimulation - they don't know *how* to be bored. Parents *do* occupy their children, but increasingly this task is left to external sources. Sadly, our children don't know how to occupy themselves without this type of stimulation - the vast majority of adults don't either. When our eyes are glued to screens and our ears listening out for messages, we're not in contact with the world itself, but rather we're living in a superficial one that we rarely disconnect from - at home, in schools, at work or when out and about; we communicate efficiently with our screens, avatar friends and followers, but rarely 'honestly' or intelligently with another human being - we tend to have an agenda if we do. We're bored with the world we live in, happily living in an artificial one and will continue to do so, until that is, we become bored with it, which I feel *certain* is on the cards. We can only be content for so long with the emptiness of monotony and the resulting mechanical minds that monotony creates; it's also only a matter of time before we realise that we're being manipulated and controlled - largely so that we don't want to, or can no longer think for ourselves - it's folly for anyone to believe that they're actually in control in this society, as long as they're flowing with the crowds.

~~~

Symptomatic of boredom is laziness, where one is disinclined to any activity - physical, mental or spiritual. Whether this is a good or bad thing is up for debate; however, I can only speak from my own perspective - understanding my own mind and purpose is an arduous enough task - it would be impossible and undesirable for me to try to understand anyone else's. As I see it, physical laziness is a symptom of boredom and can be both a good and bad thing. As a 'good' thing, lapses of activity give us time to reflect on and observe our world, undistracted by our 'usual' activities, as opposed to being bored and wondering what on earth we can do next, or who we could call and meet up with - perhaps someone equally bored. On the 'bad' side, sitting on our backsides doing nothing worthwhile at all, in front of one screen or another, becoming a so-called 'couch potato' for want of a better expression, does nothing to raise the level of our consciousness and the world's consciousness *needs* to rise - otherwise things will become increasingly grim. It's easy enough to understand how attractive being a 'couch potato' can be, arising from a general frustration with our disharmonious world - a deeply 'can't be bothered' sort of boredom that leads to a mastery *only* of mental laziness, where we can't be bothered to *think* or *even* care anymore; we become unmotivated.

On a journey of self-reflection, it's important that we begin to think about the over-debated and often unpopular subject of our spirituality - we are spiritually lazy. There are many ways in which we avoid our spiritual nature - mostly through *ad hominem* and 'straw men' arguments, because we don't want to make changes to our lives, if doing so requires any effort on our part. Examining our spiritual nature will inevitably lead to changes to our physical life. For this reason, we're more interested in finding reasons not to listen to good 'advice' than we are in following it. If we can fault the person giving the advice then that fault becomes the permission we need to ignore everything else. If we can't find the flaw in a person, we generally create one or take on board something someone else said and no matter how small the flaw we find, we hold on tightly to it. We're experts at excusing ourselves out of change.

We have neither the time, nor the inclination, to allow ourselves to be productively bored. We're constantly trying to enhance ourselves in some way by having or learning more - by becoming 'more' than we are, and certainly more than we *need* to be; what we actually get by living this way is an excess of knowledge (intellectual or otherwise) that degrades us and lowers our spirits. The knowledge we seek comes from the historical sufferings of our past, a disturbing present and an uncertain future; this leaves no room to think about 'incomprehensible metaphysical fancies' that can't be substantiated. The more we continue to behave in the way that we do, the more our heartfelt dreams will remain unfulfilled. Our minds have become dull, our brains have slowed down and our bodies slumped, because there's no motivation to change and that's a huge part of the problem. We've learnt to seek rewards for the things we invest our energy in, but they only bring temporary pleasure and we're soon searching around for something else to stimulate us. When we do what we've been conditioned to do we'll be at a loss for what to do with ourselves if there's a power cut, our internet connection is lost or our devices fail and can no longer be charged. The consequence of this is that our lives effectively come to an end, until we replace our devices or the power is restored - we're entirely addicted to our screens. I believe that if we were cut off from this electronic web, after an initial shock, we wouldn't make too much fuss about it - we'd quickly find something else to do. We're adaptable, and would learn very quickly to socialise again - perhaps even to become imaginatively bored and compassionately involved with cleaning up the mess we've created in the world, instead of finding new and ingenious ways to make more of it.

Being constructively bored is a bit of an art. It takes time to stop getting all fidgety, making another cup of tea every five minutes, feeling lonely, or reaching for the booze, other drugs, or our phones and wondering what to do with ourselves next; however, time is *all* it takes and given enough of it we learn to appreciate peace and quiet more, as our minds quieten and our bodies relax from daily stresses and excess activities - boredom becomes interesting and rewarding. At first, it's not easy to sit still and harder to be silent - so few of us are able to do it; the noise in our mind calls us back every time we try, and reminds us of all our trials and tribulations - all of our anger, emotions, failed love affairs, disappointments, jealousies, insecurities and the revenge our mind nurtures. Peace from this noise comes from observing our thoughts and seeing them for what they are - just thoughts - thoughts that have no substance in this moment, and it's 'this moment' that we gradually become more comfortable with and stimulated by. Right here and now there's only ourselves; our past is nothing more than a haunting memory of things that don't exist anymore - perhaps they never did. Ponder these things and they will become clearer and clearer as you re-train your mind to let them go. If you keep at it, sincerely, boredom will become something you welcome rather than fear.

We need to stop looking at boredom as an affliction in need of a cure, but as a cure in itself.

# Food for Thought

*When you alter something that's*
*naturally perfect, it becomes imperfect.*

Every creature on this earth needs to eat to survive and each has their own particular diet, provided by the wonderous mother nature - perfectly suited to their relative digestive systems. Of these creatures, only humans have created an industry to satisfy their growing desires and this serves several purposes. Of these, the main two are 'profit', which means sacrificing quality in order to maximise that profit and 'control', in that we've become overly dependent on industry to prepare and provide that food for us - we're fast reaching the stage where we run the risk of starving *without* this provision. We don't look after the land that could provide our food and should we be bothered to grow it for ourselves again - the majority of us wouldn't have a clue how to, let alone know how to store our crops so that they'll last all year round; also, the land has been abused to such an extent that we'd still need artificial fertilisers to stand any chance of success. If you can starve the world - you have control of it; we would do many things - that we might not ethically agree with - for money, but even more so for food. As always, I have no intention of getting into the politics or any other debate about these things, but only to look at the topic from my perspective, which I feel sure will be in line with the majority of my readers.

We take as little care of our bodies as we do our minds; both are filled - often to over-capacity - with unhealthy contents that make us ill, physically and mentally. There's no easy, kind or smooth way to put this; we eat, drink, watch and listen to junk; we, and we alone, decide what goes into our mouths! We can't treat our bodies or minds like skips and expect them to be in good health any more than we can put sub-quality fuels into the tanks of our cars and expect them to run efficiently. Health services all over the world are groaning under the strain of treating an ever-increasing number of patients with sicknesses caused by poor diet and inadequate self-care. This is well documented so I don't need to get into the details; this chapter isn't a scientific exploration of food or mental health, but rather an observatory one. I write nothing that we don't already know in our hearts, and I doubt there's a soul alive who doesn't know what 'junk food' is *or* about the threat to their health that could result from consuming it. Unfortunately, 'junk food' can be hidden by clever marketing - it's not all chips and burgers. Some products declare themselves to be healthy, yet are anything but, and they're widely available from the smallest corner shops, to the largest hypermarkets. When I go to the supermarket, I see so many customers with burgeoning trolleys of industrialised food - they buy no fresh produce whatsoever. Despite the widely publicised dangers of these 'foods' people are willing to take the risk of damaging not only their own health, but that of their families as well - most don't even take the time to read the ingredients that they're going to put into their systems. The saddest part of all this is that some fast-food outlets have queues of people waiting to buy their products, for breakfast, lunch, dinner and any snacks we care to have in-between - often with television screens to entertain us while we wait for our 'feast' - filling our minds with junk, while waiting to fill our stomachs with it.

~~~

Diets are yet another way in which we abuse ourselves. We begin them in an attempt to undo the harm done to our bodies by the food we willingly and *eagerly* eat. If the reason for our diet is to lose weight, too often we begin it with enormous enthusiasm that pays fast dividends; however, as we see the weight begin to drop off and our clothes loosen, we tend to quickly eat ourselves back into them again, because a diet is a *fad* and therefore, not a change of lifestyle - more importantly, it's not a change of mindset. The way we eat is a *habit* and too often we enjoy the excesses of this habit - not just at Christmas either. Food is a big comfort to us, as is the pleasure-bringing familiarity of the habit, and it's not just the food, but what we drink as well. We've created an array of drinks to suit every mood and palette, but the majority of them don't do our bodies any good at all. We have ice cold and boiling hot drinks, soft, alcoholic, dairy, fruity, herbal, carbonated, energy, cocktails of the above, help-you-get-to-sleep and wake-you-up drinks - drinks to stimulate, relax or stupefy us. All of these drinks contain water and water is probably the only liquid that we should be drinking - not ice cold or boiling hot either; water is what *all* other creatures in the world drink - it's nature's drink - so it must be good enough for us too.

We have many television programmes showing us how to cook our food 'correctly', with *precise* measurements and ingredients. They tell us what to cook, which drink to serve with each course, how presentable our plates should be and how to decorate the table we eat from. This is *insane*. We can buy food in any number of places, already cooked for us - from Michelin starred restaurants to greasy-spoon road-side trailers. Food is meant to sustain us - to nourish us; it is our *fuel*, but we've made a game and a huge industry out of it - an industry that causes damage to large parts of our world in the production of its 'food', so that we can eat more and more of it, particularly during our various celebrations. The pleasure foods we eat are not healthy, yet over the years we've learnt to crave them and make them rich, salty, fatty and sweeter than is good for us - it makes no sense, yet we keep on doing it. Next time you're in your local supermarket take a good look at what it's selling; the fresh produce takes up very little space compared to the industrial pre-packaged, pre-cooked, ready to heat and basically 'dead' products - if you compare them to a good home-cooked meal. I recently saw an example of processed food in my supermarket - it was called a 'Stand and Stuff Kit'; surely, industry is laughing in our faces, yet still we buy their produce. We've become lazy and dependent on society to provide our food for us; there are consequences to this change, not the least of which is the risk to our health, the health of our children and that of our planet.

There's a growing trend towards more vegetarian/vegan lifestyles and manufacturers - quick off the mark - have not missed the opportunity to produce ready meals to suit this demand. These include vegan 'cheeses', spreads, egg substitutes and imitation meats that actually 'bleed'; however, these are not necessarily beneficial to us as they're often loaded with fats, sugars, salt and other ingredients that aid in processing, prolonged shelf-life and palatability - these ingredients often include vitamins and minerals, which wouldn't need to be added if the food were wholesome.

As mentioned in my chapter 'Habits', I have been unwell and slowly but surely my health is improving. I was a vegetarian when I became ill and thought that was a good enough diet to be on, but I was wrong. I now eat a wholefood plant-based diet and never use oil in my cooking, which I always do from scratch. When I changed my diet, I cleared all non-wholefood plant-based products from my kitchen, including all oil/fat products - without sentiment or remorse - replacing them with wholesome plant-based produce. Sure, there was a learning curve, but it wasn't too steep and the internet is literally flooded with plant-based recipes that will suit any taste. I'm not saying that everyone has to change to a plant-based diet - some people thrive on other diets; for example, Dr Jordan B. Peterson eats and does well on a meat-only diet - I understand he eats *nothing* else. Where health is concerned, we need to find what works for us and to a large extent that's an individual thing.

My food tastes good, but it doesn't always give you the 'wow' factor that you might expect from a tempting slice of chocolate fudge cake or some other rich delight - a wow factor that we are addicted to - manufacturers have spent fortunes ensuring that these foods hit our 'bliss' point, so that we'll buy more of them. If you doubt this then try giving these 'treats' up for a week and see how much you miss them - *if* you actually make it through the week. I don't believe our food needs to be exciting - it needs to be nourishing and 'clean' if we're to become healthy again, and we are *not* healthy. I could go deeply into this subject, but we all know what's good for us - and what isn't - so I'll leave the medical evidence up to the doctors who have taken the time to do their own research - there are *so* many of them, like Dr John McDougall, for whom I have the greatest respect and admiration. I recommend reading his well-researched books *A Challenging Second Opinion*, and *The Starch Solution*, which delve deeply into every aspect of our health and diet, in what I consider to be a bold and beneficial way. If you don't wish to read his books, then all the information is available for *free* on his website (www.drmcdougall.com), so you don't have to lay out a single penny. *No*, I don't know him.

We've become far removed from the principle that the purpose of eating is to nourish and sustain our bodies; instead, we've turned it into a profitable business for the ever-vigilant food/media industry and an entertainment and art for ourselves. Should we choose, for example, to change to a wholefood plant-based diet, we'll come across many obstacles, like not knowing what to eat in place of the dairy and meat products we're all too familiar with. The many artificial 'substitute' products now available are *highly* processed and replacing the 'real thing' with them doesn't change our mindset at all; we create the *same* meals with them, and consequently, believe them to be healthy alternatives - we might just as well eat the *real thing*, for clearly, that's still our intention. If we decide to change our diets, we *must* also change our mindset for the results to be truly effective, and this involves separating ourselves from the mindset that eats for pleasure, to the mindset that eats *with* pleasure, but also intelligence - highly processed vegan food is just as bad for us as the products that it's attempting to replace. It's not intelligent to eat food that we know harms us, even if it *does* give us pleasure - often that harm will manifest in the future and because we don't see it now, we ignore it; we may after all, not be alive tomorrow; there are so many ways in which we don't care about the things we may not live to experience, even the futures of our own children. We need to learn to care about our bodies and what food we choose to put into them; when we do this, our food will *care* for us - it won't necessarily allow us to live longer, but it will improve the quality of our life, our overall wellbeing, and quite possibly avoid certain debilitating illnesses altogether. We also need to learn to care about what's being fed into our minds; for example, from television, radio, newspapers, friends, acquaintances, teachers etc.; if it makes you feel bad, then it *is* bad. If *we* don't care about what we feed our bodies *and* minds, we can't in good conscience, expect others to.

# We are One

*We are all One - humanity. We may not like certain aspects of this, just as we may not like the nose on our faces; however, it remains a part of us, whether we like it or not.*

If you've ever seen a large mosaic, on a wall or floor for example, you'll know that to appreciate it fully you have to stand well back - otherwise you'll only see a small part of it. What the whole picture represents gradually reveals itself as we distance ourselves from it, and it's possible, if it's a large enough mosaic, that we couldn't get far enough away to see it all from one point; we'd have to change our position many times in order to take in different aspects of it - we could never see the 'whole' picture at once. Society *is* such a mosaic and it's a highly complicated multi-dimensional one - it's *enormous*; we are but a single tile of it, surrounded by a grout moat of 'I' 'Me' 'My' thinking. We live in a world where our focus is on ourselves, so we're unable to see the structure of society or the part we play in it. Just as with the mosaic, we have to pull away before we can hope to understand even a tiny part of the picture that we're an intrinsic part of - the picture that we too often attempt to insulate ourselves from and consequently, we remain isolated from various truths behind our protective walls/covers of illusion.

We live in a world where our focus is on ourselves, on the 'I', so we're unable to see the structure of society or the part we play in it.

We have to shift our focus from the 'I' to the whole of 'SOCIETY' to see it clearly. When we do this, although 'I' is at the centre, it's plain to see that it's no more important than any other letter.

From my perspective, if humanity's focus was on a philosophy of what's best for *everyone*, the world would become a wiser place. Through that wisdom we would eradicate wars, racism, sexism, confusion, hatred, destruction and all other forms of 'evil'. It's not lost on me that this is stating the obvious, but as it's so obvious, I'm left asking 'Why haven't we done it?' You may have other ideas about how to create a sane society through the economy, force, restrictions, laws or even by keeping the population 'stoned' as in Aldous Huxley's *A Brave New World*. Perhaps I stopped you with my use of the word 'evil' - I know of no other word to describe the horrors we inflict on each other, or the many forms of separation we've created between us. The potential for evil lies within each of us and in my opinion, evil is not a winged, horned or trident-wielding beast; it's the absence of 'good'. Evil is doing something that harms another - inflicted through thought, violence, ignorance, judgement or verbal abuse, to ourselves or any other living creature; we've been doing it throughout human history and there's little evidence of any willingness to change; on the contrary, things are 'heating up'.

If we don't make wisdom our highest priority, we'll continue to live in a state of fear - a fear of impending disaster and an increasingly totalitarian society, which is where we're currently heading at full speed; it would be unwise to doubt it. We are copycats; that is to say we follow examples - that's how we learnt everything we already know (or think we know). When we learn by example, it's important that the example be 'good'. Our governments are corrupt - they always have been;

imagine the influence that this corruption has on us - we are none of us so innocent. An open-minded glance at our influences (local or distant) quickly reveals where we get all our information from; the internet, our peers, our idols, books, television, newspapers, etc. The news is always bad and therefore, that's the energy we pick up and that's what we create in society; although we know that a lot of what we see and hear about isn't entirely true, we tend to take it on board and *make* it true - especially if it's expedient to do so. If more individuals held wisdom as their highest dream then the effect would spread throughout society at all levels, but as long as we 'go with the flow', evident everywhere, we're heading for more of the same. Every individual has an effect on the whole and even if that effect is tiny, it can make a difference. Imagine a tiny splinter stuck in your finger; it can cause so much pain that it interferes with your daily activities, but when that splinter is removed so is the pain along with it. Tempering our thoughts and actions with wisdom brings many benefits that don't need to be enumerated; there's no 'fallout' that needs to be fixed from a wise decision.

There's a tendency to blame 'society' for our woes - as though 'society' were nothing to do with us - and accept that we're an immutable product of it. In this way, we insulate ourselves from any responsibility concerning it. The fact remains, however, that all of us make up society and the things we do have a knock-on effect. By the same token, the things we *don't* do also have a knock-on effect. Obviously, a tiny baby born into dire circumstances is not responsible for his dilemma, but there comes a time when he can take responsibility from then on - make decisions and steer his own life; I know this for a fact as I was one of those babies. Whether or not my circumstances were due to some past life's karma is up for debate and though this idea can be rationalised out, it can't be proven. Showing you that 'we are One' is difficult because understanding the concept comes only after many years of sincere self-reflection - drilling as deeply into our minds as we possibly can and watching our thoughts and dreams in action. As we reflect on society and our place in it, it becomes clear that we are one and the same. 'Me' becomes 'We' when we make a decision to turn our lives around.

We're two weeks into 2019 as I write this and a day after the 'celebrations' I was in a local town; the filth left on the pavements and streets was horrible - food, vomit, etc., and it was raining; consequently, the pavements were slippery and treacherous to walk on. Those who left the mess have in all probability forgotten about it; the following day they were in all likelihood laughing/sleeping it off - they'll not take the time to take responsibility for their actions and I doubt they'd consider returning to clear up the mess; someone could be injured, someone *else* has to clean it up, the energy of the town was 'low' - we leave things in our wake that have a knock-on effect on others and *that* makes us One - *society*; what others do affects us and what we do affects others. A smile can be infectious; whatever we leave behind directly affects others and when we become truly aware of that fact, the knock-on effect is that we become responsible for our actions. As that awareness and responsibility unfold, we endeavour to leave only good in our wake. Taken to another level, the actions of our governments affect us; whatever they do, someone, somewhere is paying the price for it. Now, don't get me wrong, there's a lot of good in society too, but it's not always apparent and tends to be swept under the carpet as we watch more and more chaos unfold.

# Don't Get Me Started!

I love walking early in the mornings - anytime from around 4 a.m. if I'm up and about, which I usually am. When the stars are out, on a dark night, I'm able to see what we know as the Milky Way; I feel small, vulnerable and as though I were the only person in the universe. I'm standing on a planet - at least that's what I've been conditioned to believe - with nothing but open space all around me; there's nothing between the stars and me. It's at times like these that I wonder where, or even *if*, I actually am; space is huge, and I'm at the centre of it - it's not within my power to know any more than that. For all I know, I might be living under a dome with stars painted on the roof; this whole thing called 'life' could be an enormous hoax - not knowing for certain is where the magic moments lie; they reside between what we think we know and what we don't - between the lines of text. It's a mystery, a wonder and I *know* that I'm meant to be in awe of it - I *am* in awe of it. I also know that at my current level of consciousness there's no choice but to live in either 'awe' of limitless possibility, or a state of frustration, fear and limitation. If life is a hoax, then someone or something must have instigated it; develop that thought and regardless of what life is or isn't, something amazing is waiting for us and I believe we have to prepare ourselves for it - just as we have to prepare for anything we choose to do during the course of our lifetimes; for example, an exam, a job interview or even a picnic.

Some mornings I wake up feeling disorientated; I don't know if I'm actually awake or still dreaming. This morning I woke from a dream where - on seeing something horrific - I was telling the people in my dream that "This *can't* be real - it *has* to be a dream"; it was a powerful and disturbing dream, but I was unable to make it lucid. The people in my dream never responded; they were emotionless, stood staring at me and were no threat whatsoever. I can relate all parts of the dream to events from the previous day and without going into any details, I can tell you it was pretty weird with an unpleasant ending. Not because anything unpleasant happened to me during the previous day, but because my mind twisted everything out of proportion and made something ugly out of it - our minds are in the habit of doing that. The gap between the dream and waking states feels like it's closing. When I go to sleep I slip into dreams filled with whatever I'm thinking about at the time, or whatever I did, watched or talked about during the day; as is the case with dreams, there's no time or space and consequently, they're all muddled - I don't tend to dream of anything in my distant past anymore. I see our dreams as 'leaks' from an overfilled convoluted mind that's trying to make sense of the world - they're a form of housekeeping. I'm living in a strange place where I can't be sure of anything at all, not even if I'm really 'here'. After many years of sincere self-reflection, I now see the world from a distance and from that distance things have become clearer, including the fact that we've no idea who we really are, where we are or what happens 'next'; there are plenty of theories, scientific and otherwise, but none can be substantiated from our limited position of ignorance in the universe - we can but wonder at the marvel of the mysterious circumstances we find ourselves in.

I've often felt lost in this world; actually, I think I feel it all the time. I don't believe there's anyone who honestly feels any different. Aren't we, after all, every one of us trying to find our place in the world - our homely and comfortable niche, or if you prefer, somewhere to belong? Well, that implies 'lost' doesn't it? We try so hard to fit in, but we never can, because the way society is structured brings only suffering and illness. There are those who try hard to overturn the system and they dedicate their lives to the task; sadly, they're few and far between. Society doesn't feel like a natural or healthy environment to me, and quite obviously it isn't, or there wouldn't be so much hardship and insanity in it. My father used to say that I have to make something of myself, as though I weren't something to begin with, and this sort of encouragement left me feeling inadequate; he used to drum that message in, and as a result, I felt like a stranger in a world that didn't know I existed. I wanted to be allowed to be myself - I still do, but this - according to my father - wasn't going to be good enough, and wouldn't turn me into a 'useful' addition to society. I was always the philosophical type - so I hated school and felt it had nothing to teach me about life or myself.

My youth was spent feeling like an alien, in a world I didn't belong to; I never knew then that it was *my* world and that I had to make something of it, rather than have it make something of me.

As I see it, society is largely soulless and this is a sad state of affairs - a great many of us have become increasingly self-centred and lacking in compassion for the rest of mankind. I live my life more and more in my home, as here - with my partner - I can make a little sense of things. Although I'm at home a lot, I know I'm not missing out on anything. Sometimes, I feel as though I've moved into the wilderness and wonder if I'll remain in it for the rest of my life. Apart from going out on my walks (locally or to the beach), shopping, dental or medical appointments or popping into a friend's for a cup of tea, I've no wish to leave my home; this doesn't mean that I wouldn't do something impulsive, like jump on a plane to Portugal or Italy for a week if the idea took my fancy, but for now the 'adventure' holds little appeal. At home, I can think in peace and quiet and watch the comings and goings of my thoughts with increasing interest and attention; I've learnt to enjoy doing this, but I'm still surprised by some of the thoughts that pop up out of the blue; it seems I'm still attached to some of them, though I like to believe that I'm not. I spend a great deal of time writing, editing, illustrating and reading, and I like life that way; the more I delve into myself, the less of my*self* there is to delve into. I feel an increasing need to justify my existence - to myself that is; there's no point in living if I don't do something meaningful with my life - if I don't *grow*; I can't live in a perfunctory fashion - I did that, albeit reluctantly, for long enough. Now that this book is almost finished - it's my 7$^{th}$ - I'm thinking to myself 'What shall I do next?' and so far I have no answer to this question.

From my distant viewpoint, the whole world is buying and selling something, *anything* it can, whether it be for pennies or pounds - there's something for every pocket; money is our god and we seek it more than we do 'peace on earth'. We rape the earth of its materials, and sell them on in either the same form, or a new material that science has created - the most damaging of which - to the best of my limited knowledge - is plastic; we're drowning in the stuff. We make a penny anyway we can, regardless of ethics, morals or consequences. Industry produces whatever we want it to and when we no longer have a use for it, we sell it on or throw it out; a huge industry has been born from our disposals - our waste is big business. Where there's a demand, there's a supply - remove the demand and you remove that supply. Society, worldwide, works as a *whole* - it always has and always will. Can you imagine the good we could do with this knowledge, if we put aside our desire for more and more products - and for more and more profit? What *is* profit after all - isn't it simply excess to requirements? The sickness to buy and sell has literally spread everywhere; people who make videos for our information or entertainment now want us to financially support them, so that they'll continue to make them - before they did it for pleasure, exposure and for subscribers, but as they grew so did the knowledge that they could profit from their enterprise and in some cases, give up their jobs;

donation requests to these channels is at pandemic levels and it will have to stop somewhere, sooner or later; Everyone wants their 'cut of the action' and we can't afford to support them all, without doing more damage to the world than we have already.

Although I'm not exactly a recluse, society offers little that interests me. I'm neither left nor right; I've no fixed views on politics, science, history or any other nonsense that we're only privy to a tiny part of - we're fed only crumbs and scramble for them thinking that we're being adequately nourished. Socialising doesn't interest me too much either, as I simply don't think in the same way others do. It's difficult to know the things I do, and listen to people talking about worldly affairs in the same way that I've heard about them all of my life - talking about the same things, with different people playing the same parts, as though there were something new to be discussed. In many ways, I know when people are lying to me, when they're kidding themselves, when they're hurting and don't want to admit it - sometimes I even know what they're thinking; this makes socialising difficult, as I don't like to contradict people, yet at the same time I'm living in a different world to them. For some time now I've understood - with clarity - the term 'silence is golden'. So as far as possible, I keep myself to myself.

It's hard to live for a purpose that we can't be certain exists (something beyond our deaths), which is why many people live what I can only describe as nihilistic lifestyles; rushing here and there before they run out of time and energy - enthusiastically chasing any dream that's put in front of them. I see so many unhappy faces when I'm out and about and this leaves me sad, because I know they could be happier if they knew the things I know. As a whole, our education needs to change because if it doesn't, we'll go on and on hurting and harming each other, as we always have done. Isn't discovering this fact the point of history and our museums, both of which are filled with the horrors of our pasts - how we wreak havoc on the world - and I for one am weary of them. It's not all nasty, but those things are at the forefront of our learning. I remember learning about Henry VIII when I was at school, and how he cut off the heads of his wives - I was very disturbed by this; we need to move on from these things if society is ever to become intelligent and sane; just as with the memories and suffering that torture us while we're trying to get to sleep, we have to let them go if we're to grow. Children do not need to walk on the blood-ridden paths of our ancestors, they need to be taught to have respect and compassion for all things and to create for the *good* of mankind, not its detriment. Things in the outside world aren't going to change until *we* do; just like a snake, we need to shed our old skin - with all its parasites - and reveal what lies beneath it - a new skin; we need to alter our mindset if we're ever to transcend insanity.

Change won't be made at the 'top' and we seriously need to recognise this. Those at the top aren't going to change their ways at our insistence - they like things just the way they are and they're going to make our lives tougher still - evidence for this is all around us. Change must grow from the bottom up - our youths are our future leaders and they can make a difference if they're taught to live intelligently; they need to be taught to have compassion for others and to spend less time on vain and foolish unattainable dreams - they need to see that they're destroying their own world, and to care about that. We must all do our bit to help this process evolve; mine, it seems, is to write my books and hope that they don't fall on deaf ears. At the end of the day we have to become responsible for ourselves - something greatly lacking in society; through that responsibility comes psychological growth, through that growth compassion and through that compassion less frustration, less selfishness and a greater ability to see life from a distance. From that distance we realise that we: can't change the whole, can't change another human being, rely less on society, fear less, grow in stature, grow in wisdom, respect ourselves and elevate our consciousness level; I'd suggest that it's a desirable package, with fringe benefits, *and* also that we *can* take it with us when we leave this world, unlike our physical 'trophies'. The world we live in is the result of our complacency and ignorance (ignorance meaning 'to ignore'). If you believe in nothing after this life then that's a great waste of a life and a shame, but even if there exists in you a tiny element of doubt, then surely it's worth preparing for.

# Authority

*If we won't control ourselves,*
*then we will be controlled.*

Once we start thinking seriously about any given
subject, things we didn't see before become
apparent - things that, for 'societal' convenience, we
pushed to the back of our minds. When looking at
'authority' for example, it's possible to see that we're not
the ones who are in control of our lives - even though
each one of us would like to believe that we are; we were
all born under the 'authority' of another - a *corrupt* other.
So what is authority? It's the power given to another to
control - by both allowing and prohibiting the actions
of others. The problem is that we never, as far as is
possible to know, gave anyone else the authority to rule
over us; this knowledge implies that control of our lives
was taken from ourselves and our ancestors - we were
born into a long-established control system. Realising
this began in me a process of reflecting on how much
my life was, and to some extent still is, controlled by
the authority of others - legal systems, governments,
religions, and other closer to home influences. We can
choose whether or not to interact with these 'authorities'
and tend to meet them when we're, for example, in
trouble of some kind, in need of a sympathetic ear, need

permission to do something, someone to lean on, or someone to blame for our woes.

Do we need authoritative figures in our lives? That's a complicated question and can be answered only by each of us, as an individual. Society, in its current mindset, would collapse into anarchy without authority; as it did for example, during the Murray-Hill riot in Montreal in 1969 when the police force went on strike - resulting in chaos. Without law enforcement there will be social unrest, until such time as we take responsibility for the way we interact with the world and each other. In other words, when we gain a 'healthy' authority over ourselves and our base instincts to 'riot', for example, we'll not need to be governed; however, as long as we rely on someone else to control us and that *that* 'someone else' is as psychologically unhealthy as we are, there'll be corruption and chaos. Staying with the riot theme, there are always more rioters than there are police officers and in order for them not to be overpowered, law enforcement has to be strict and tough - the more we misbehave, the more law 'enforcement' will be imposed, which can lead to only one destination - totalitarianism.

Where does Authority and its power originate? We're taught from a young age to accept authority without question - the authority of our parents, teachers and in general, our elders. This authority leaves us without a say in the world, until such time as we're considered to be old enough to live our own lives - wisely or otherwise - and even then few of us actually have a say in anything at all - authority is wielded over us from every angle in the form of propaganda, coercion, force, peer pressure, etc.

We're surrounded by authority in films, advertisements, news stories, books, music, games, soap operas, game shows, and in many more ways. Authority not only controls us, but it influences our thoughts, behaviour, beliefs and prejudices - it steers us into our futures; consequently, it shapes us into the person we are and are 'destined' to be for the rest of our lives - if we can think it, we've been influenced by it! Authority is a little like water; it's pure until it has been contaminated, and it *has* been contaminated for a long time now. Why do we obey our tainted authorities? Because our parents did (and still do), and *their* parents before them; most of all, we obey because we're afraid not to - no matter what the consequences. In our society, keeping safe and secure is Item One on the agenda - not only for ourselves, but for our 'authority figures' too.

What exactly is it we're trying to keep safe and secure from? Pain? Suffering? Death? To feel threatened by pain or suffering is to acknowledge the overwhelming power we've given to our authorities; to feel threatened by death is surely the highest form of delusion.

They say 'you can run, but you can't hide'; we can't get away from authority - it's right there when we need to interact with the world in any way, like a dark hovering cloud … waiting to rain on us should we dare to step out of line. Our world can't be escaped from - we have nowhere else to go, so it would be a good idea to live in it intelligently, as opposed to recklessly, because we can't go on doing what we're doing to our world for much longer. Authority, even if we refuse to acknowledge that it *exists*, will *always* exist in our world, until such time as we become an authority unto ourselves. At the lowest level of authority, in society, we have the eldest child of a family looking after their siblings; they're just children themselves and therefore unqualified to wield authority over others. At the highest level of authority in our society are the corporations (perhaps they also answer to someone) - I don't need to get into any details about such a well-known subject; however, sooner or later they themselves must answer to a higher authority; there's no escape for *any* of us.

When authority is imposed on us, it's never an 'authentic' authority - bullies impose authority on others. Imposed authority instils fear and creates resentment; if fear needs to be instilled in the population then something's intrinsically wrong with that authority - at all levels. Authority leads to the suppression of the masses who live beneath it and *challenge* it - it's the masses that allow authority to grow stronger and remain on its pedestal. On the other hand, what would we do without our authorities? In our current mindset there would be chaos, as with the 'Murray-Hill' unrest in Montreal, or 'May 1968' in France, so authority is absolutely necessary to keep us in line - not solely for the advancement of an agenda to totally control us, but also to protect us from ourselves; imagine, if you will, a classroom full of children after the teacher has left the room for a few minutes. Not all the 'powers that be' are 'evil' - some have our best interests at heart, but until *we* have our best interest at heart we'll remain as we are - confused, suffering, living in fear, separated, judgemental and looking for someone to blame for our predicament.

We're affected by authority every moment of our lives - by purchasing a fashionable or advertised product, by stopping at a road junction before we cross it, paying bills or being afraid to stand up for what we *truly* believe in. It's difficult to get away from our conditioning and the expectations of others; I have a friend who once said to me 'You *always* have to be different', but I don't *try* to be different - I *am* different and I like it better than being 'the same'; we are none of us the same and life would be rather pointless and trite if we were. We have different appearances, different experiences, different voices, different dreams and our own unique fingerprints - we were never meant to be clones of one another, but we *are* one and share one world together. Society teaches us about 'equality', but we're not psychologically equal at all; some will kill, some won't, some reflect on their lives and humanity as a whole and some don't, some live intelligently and some don't. We're all at different stages of awareness, whether we like it or not, and that's okay - it's just the way things are and we have to go with the flow of it all. The greatest effect that authority has over us is that it removes the need - and will - for us to be our *own* authority.

Authority over ourselves is *not* achieved by living according to a set of our *own* standards that we never waver from - though in many ways we all subconsciously do this, and not always in the best interest of ourselves or others; however, at the core of each of us is something essentially 'good' that would never harm another, *including* ourselves, and for me this is the *only* 'true' authority - anything else is a corruption and there's a lot of corruption in our world - not just in governments, but in our own hearts too; we're all too frequently immune to the suffering of others - evident not only in our actions, but by our deepest thoughts.

Evil = the absence of good

Good = the absence of evil = 'true' authority.

What 'true' authority is *not* is a 'free for all' mentality where each of us has the right to do whatever we want - a sort of 'up yours' attitude to everyone else, which means to ourselves too; there's far too much of this happening in society and it doesn't do us any good whatsoever - on the contrary, we're harming anything that can be harmed, and we're going at it with tremendous enthusiasm, despite the fact that it will inevitably lead to our destruction - we're actively *waiting* for it and in some cases shouting out 'Bring it on'. Gaining authority over ourselves is not something that can be 'permitted' to happen through any form of legislation - banning this and banning that, standing for this or standing for that - it's something that we *have* to work at and the *only* way to do this is through self-reflection - with the intention of being the best person we can be to ourselves and others - it takes time and sincerity. When we see that we harm ourselves every day, and begin to care about it, it motivates us to stop doing those things; like eating food with no nutritional value, staying up late, drinking to excess, smoking, overindulging in other unhealthy pastimes, looking down on others or following new trends - these things harm us physically and psychologically.

True authority comes with the removal of the conditioning imposed on us since we were infants - it requires a new start, a new heart and a clear unbiased mind towards everything and everyone. Can you imagine that - it would be like being born again and having control over our choices from the beginning of that birth - no influence, dogma or ritual; to some that would be an impossible state of mind to achieve, but to me ... well I just keep on going, because there's nothing else in this world worth striving for and nothing else that I consider worth expending my energy on. We can't be so 'free' when our bodies are born - we're surrounded by too much established influence, but we can remove that influence once we see it for what it is, and understand how it has shaped our beliefs and characters; it then becomes possible to understand how influence has shaped the world.

To become our own authority we must first 'realise' that our character was formed by various influences; we need to realise that the character doesn't belong to us and has nothing at all to do with what lies at the heart of each and every one of us - then and only then do we begin to change. Self-observation reveals much if we're prepared to be completely honest about what we find during our enquiry; for example, by making no more excuses about why we behave the way we do and why we can't change - this is self-deceptive and self-destructive; our mind loves to play along with these objectives, and it will continue to do so as long as we allow it to. To benefit from self-observation we have to catch thoughts at their onset, before they develop into full-blown dramas - recognise the birth of each thought, watch it without judgement and see that, when left unfertilised, the thoughts fade away like a dream. We need to peel away our layers of bias, beliefs, rituals and other influences that we identify as 'us', if we wish to rise above them - they belong to a low level of consciousness and only serve to perpetuate the walls we've so ingeniously constructed and placed between us. To become our own authority, it's important to realise that we *never* were in control of our lives - even though most of us wouldn't care to admit it.

Our judgements aren't only manifested in our thoughts, but also in our actions. Watch every step you take, slow the process down and you'll begin to recognise certain patterns in your behaviour; we become our own authority when we make the decision to change these patterns - when we don't like what we see in ourselves or when we don't accept the mould that society has pressed us into. Take for example, your thoughts when approaching other people; instead of criticising them or seeing their faults, see them as having suffered in life as much, if not more, than you have and that that suffering has made them into who they are now; fearful, disheartened and incomplete, in much the same way that we all are - we're not so different. If we do this often enough we develop empathy and compassion for others and consequently, have no need or will to judge or condemn them - rather than avoid them, where possible, we do what we can to help. I could tell you how putting this into action has changed me, but not in any way that you'll fully understand until you experience it for yourself; somehow, it lightens the heart and the burden we all carry and *this* is surely worth our time and energy.

What we're all searching for can't be given to us by an outside authority - few of us even know what it is we're searching for, but we do know that we can't find it in our corrupt society. When our influences are corrupt, our behaviour will be too and it's up to us to see society for what it is; we can see this clearly when we step away from it and see it as a whole - not just in our community, but worldwide; the patterns reveal themselves when we're willing to look at them. The very action of stepping back a little begins the process of becoming our own authority - our psychological growth for *good*. Authority of ourselves doesn't mean ignoring or disobeying the 'powers that be' or encouraging others to do so - in some cases this would be nothing more than rebellion; however, it doesn't mean obeying everything we're told either, especially when it's not in our best interest or the best interests of others - some rules are foolish and detrimental to humanity. Becoming our own authority means taking responsibility for ourselves and actions by keeping a check on ourselves, emotionally and psychologically - minute by minute; it's a process that leads to further and higher questions, when we're ready to ask them. By becoming our own authority we're no longer prey to the changing winds of society; we march to our own drum and in this way become a wiser person, and a world of wise people can only be a good thing.

To reiterate …

Evil = the absence of good

Good = the absence of evil = 'true' authority

~~~

Love = the absence of both good *and* evil

# Mindset

*The seeds planted in our minds are what*
*create our mindset - how they develop*
*depends entirely on how we nurture them.*

It's a curious thing, the word 'set'. It serves as a stand-alone word, a prefix and a suffix, yet whichever is used it conveys the sense of something final, or possibly just beginning. The concrete, or jelly, has set. All set? A setback. A full set. A set idea. To be set on something. Set in stone? No doubt you'll know many more situations where that small three-lettered word 'set' can be used - one that's of great interest to me is 'mindset', or if you will, a set mind. I think of a mindset as rather like a collection of something; say for example, cards. When you have all the cards you have a set; within that set are other sets, such as a set of clubs or diamonds - when you take one away from the deck or the 'club' set, it's no longer complete; if you add a card there are a whole set of other problems that can result from it. But of course, thought is much more complicated than cards and unlike a deck of cards, our mindset *can* be altered - a new thought can override an existing one; we *can* have a change of mind.

A mindset exists where we refuse to accept, or haven't considered, that there may be an alternative - we're set in our ways. Why might we do this? Tradition? Pride?

Stubbornness? Boredom? Fear? Laziness? A mind 'set' is a 'closed' mind, self-limiting and therefore unlikely to change; some people are happy to remain with this state of mind - it fosters security instead of uncertainty, but there's no vitality in that attitude. However, sometimes a change of mindset may be forced on us by a life-changing situation; for example, by an accident or the death of someone close to us - forcing us to re-evaluate our lives; sometimes something beautiful can be born from these painful experiences. An open mind copes far easier with changes in its circumstances than a mind set in its ways. Re-evaluating our life doesn't necessarily require a dramatic incident, but can be brought about by our own thoughts - the penny dropping - when we allow ourselves to consider possible alternatives to our mindset; a revelation, if you like - often when we're caught off-guard and a particular belief is newly challenged or demolished; for example, when a person we least expect it from proffers an act of kindness to us.

On our journey down this so-called 'narrow road' it becomes difficult to verbalise not only the things that change our way of thinking - our mindset - but also our world view. We can't quite put our finger on why or how this occurs or in what way the change - or 'phenomenon' - manifests itself, but it *is* there, like something seen out of the corner of our eye. Our cultural environment created our mindset and this is true for *everyone*, no matter where we live in the world; we can have no thoughts or beliefs that haven't been planted in our mind by society, and the society that planted them is unhealthy, to say the least. This realisation can be hard to come to terms with - in some of us, resistance to it can be fierce, and in my case I found it quite sickening; it left me feeling utterly lost, with no-one to turn to and nothing to trust in. We love to think that we're individual, but whatever we prefer, think, believe, or try to change about ourselves was once implanted in our mind. So thought is the culprit of our predicament and as our thoughts have been manipulated since our birth, it follows that whatever we 'think' must always be 'old news' - there's nothing new to be discovered in our society; we do, in fact, live through past experiences - our own and those of others.

We are but scatterlings - lost in a wilderness full of misleading information that comes from others with benevolent or in some cases, malevolent intentions; some come from a position of ignorance and others from one of intelligence. Some, with malintent believe they know what's best for the rest of us - some with good intentions actually do us and our home planet a lot of harm and some prevent us from harming ourselves; despite appearances, society is balanced - albeit unevenly. A little thought into these matters reveals the knowledge that we're powerless to fight the human battle with each other - particularly with the upper echelons of society. My mindset is mine, yours is yours and theirs is theirs - we can't change each other because none of us wishes to be changed. Our mind is *set* and it will remain that way until we decide to be more flexible about how we look at the world and each other; looking at the 'whole' human condition is the only way to allow order to tame and placate the chaos of our minds and though it seems to be unfair, the change must take place within ourselves.

We've *all* been conditioned, but it's our personal experiences that shape us into the person we've become; your experiences are different to mine, as is the environment you grew up in, so it follows that your character, memories and resulting biases are also different. Those in the upper echelons have also been conditioned, but they serve society in different ways to the majority of people; in a nutshell, some of us are conditioned to lead, some to manage and some to follow; the system is both ancient and solid, making it immoveable by any one individual - it's just the way things are and the world will continue to be this way whether we like it or not. No matter how loudly we protest, our voices are like waves crashing on the beach, rapidly replaced by another, leaving no visible sign of our having been there at all - yet still we shout out. The system is like that of social media; our posts disappear under a foray of others, never to be seen again, if in fact they ever were and regardless of this knowledge we continue to post them.

Once we become aware of how set in our ways we are, the possibility of change opens up to us and this can be an exciting time, if change is what we want. We don't have to change of course - we may be quite happy where we are; however, having the option is liberating because we can think to ourselves 'I don't *have* to do this', but it suits me for now. For some people the idea of change is terrifying - even though they're unhappy in their lives, it's a comfortable and familiar unhappiness; their mindset is on rails and they don't relish the thought of change. If you're like me however, beneficial change is always welcome. Sometimes we have to *dare* to make changes and at other times their forced upon us. First and foremost, if we truly want change, we must realise that there are things we can change, and things we can't; so many people continue to try to change the things that can't be changed (often other people) and this exercise will never bear fruit.

Changing our mind takes time; we don't become a different person overnight. We have more than one mindset and therefore, more than one way in which we can experience change. Say for example a person has never eaten Indian food and says they find it distasteful, even though they've never tried it; one day they try it and become fans of the food. Personally, as a child I used to hate vegetables - largely because I hated the way they were cooked, but over the years I've learnt to cook them in ways that please me and they no longer turn my stomach - on the contrary, I love them now. It was my willingness to try them in different ways that changed my mind about them; I could have stuck to my guns and missed out on the delicious varieties of meals that I now enjoy. However, these are trivial matters in comparison to some of the bigger things in life. If I were asked what societal mindset I'd like to change, it would be that *everyone* sees *everyone* as the 'human race', thus eradicating the 'my family', 'my religion', 'my country' and any other 'my' mindset that fractures and separates humanity *from itself*.

~~~

As mentioned at the beginning of this chapter, a mindset is a collection of thoughts; we need to change those thoughts so that our mindset is one that benefits ourselves and our planet in some way - our thoughts need not be set in stone, no matter how hard life's hammer and chisel hits us. We need to think about how we treat people in general, so that we become welcoming and friendly to those we encounter outside of social or family circles, even if they can be exasperating. Our mindset needs to become one of benevolence to others and if we have that mindset, we're more likely to meet 'kindred spirits' - slowly changing and improving our own lives and along the way, if that's our purpose, the lives of others. However, I recognise that changing my mindset is not going to do much for the world itself, but I also know that over the years I've become a better and stronger person; for a start, I like myself more than I used to and that was definitely a mindset worth changing. Personal growth comes with a change of mind and if we don't change our minds we'll remain rooted to the spot like a tree - we are not trees; we are people and capable of change. There's so much we're missing out on by not 'uprooting' ourselves and changing our perspective. Peace of mind comes to us when we change our mind and until we do, the things that bring stress and anxiety into our lives - such as sorrow, anger, regret, hatred, judgement, jealousy and revenge, will continue to consume us; they are highly toxic to our minds and damaging to ourselves, and to others.

## Parting Thoughts

*Live thoughtfully, and do no harm.*

When I first started this journey, I was like a squash ball bouncing around the court - ideas and realisations energised me so much that I could hardly contain them; I was on a mission, or if you prefer, an 'evangelical' crusade; I wanted to share my experiences with *everyone*, and for them to become as fired up and excited as I was. They didn't, which I found somewhat puzzling - often exasperating. It soon became apparent that this journey, my journey, was for *me* and *me* alone.

Naturally, the frisson I first felt couldn't last forever - it never does; the initial excitement of discovery soon fades and settles into a more manageable flow - now I take things more slowly, as they come - one day at a time, one experience at a time. Dismantling ourselves is never easy, and it would be wise to doubt anyone who tells you otherwise. Our thoughts, hopes, aspirations, intentions, motives - everything that makes up 'Me', are laid bare under the examiner's gaze - in this case, mine; what we discover can be surprising, if not a bit shocking. There's no getting away from ourselves - however hard we may try; there's always that voice that cries out 'FRAUD!' when we attempt it.

The society we're born into is mischievous and inhospitable - it doesn't have our best interest at heart and as we grow older, we don't have *its* best interest at heart either; the evidence for this is all around us. Something has to budge if we're to grow, psychologically, and that 'budge' has to come from deep within us. There's *no-one* that can change us unless we *want* to be changed - we're *that* obstinate and bloody-minded - often seeking that which we think we need, rather than what we *truly* need. This is our habitual lifestyle and it's a difficult habit to break, but that doesn't mean it can't be achieved. What's needed is a change of mind *and* a change of heart. One way to do this is to remove ourselves from unhealthy relationships that drag us down and make us feel bad about ourselves; it's better to have no friends at all, or family for that matter, than to remain in a situation that leaves us feeling low, unappreciated, used, abused or invaluable. we have to start caring, at first for ourselves, and *only* then will we become able to *genuinely* care for others.

~~~

Isn't it worth a little of our time to think about what happens to us after we die? My thoughts on death, at the moment, are that although our bodies most certainly die, our mindset remains with us. This is important to realise if we don't wish to continue repeating what we've always done - possibly I've been doing just that for thousands of years - perhaps millions - and frankly, that's long enough. I feel it's time for me to move on from this plane - to cease wasting my energy on things that don't matter and to concentrate on the more important things of life, for as long as I may live; this

I've promised myself. My wish is to *grow* - to leave this life at a higher level of consciousness than when I came into it, transcending this existence, or as some put it, to climb out of this 'river of life'. If I don't 'grow', then my life has been completely wasted.

There are as many thoughts on what happens after death as there are people thinking them, but they essentially fall into two groups: that there's 'nothing' or that there's 'something' - either way it's a win-win situation, but that's a rather cynical way of examining the meaning of our lives. As we can't prove either scenario, wouldn't it be better to live our lives as though there were 'something', and to see that what we do now has a bearing on that hereafter. In this way we'd benefit from a higher mindset now, which may carry over into whatever - if anything - comes next. If we must strive for anything at all, then I'd suggest it's to become a '24 carat' human being with all that that implies - you can be certain that few of us - if any - are genuine. I'd suggest that these thoughts are worth pondering over - for who knows, we may have to answer 'then' for our 'now' - if not to a higher authority, then at the very least to ourselves.

We each have to make our own minds up about whether or not a higher authority exists, and that task is best done through self-reflection, rather than through the thoughts, fears, dogmas and conditioning of ourselves or someone else. To doubt *all* that we've been taught creates a healthy mind and to achieve this is to become our *own* judge and jury. To doubt is to plant a new seed, and a healthy mind grows from nurturing that seed - allowing it to grow in a natural and organic way, without the influence or direction of anyone else. Slowly, but surely, we become a mystery to ourselves; a lovely mystery without fear or judgement of the irrational world we find ourselves living in.

Though some might find it morbid, I have to admit to feeling more than a little excited about what comes next, and when the time comes, I pray that I'm adequately prepared for it.

*And so you see I have come to doubt*
*All that I once held as true.*
*I stand alone without beliefs.*
*The only truth I know is you.*

- Paul Simon

# NOTES

# NOTES

# NOTES

# NOTES

# NOTES

## About the Author

Renée Paule was born in London and was brought up in an orphanage, despite having two living parents. Subjected to mental and physical cruelty, the trauma she suffered left her with twelve years of almost total amnesia. Six marriages later (four official), she chose to 'take stock' and began a process of questioning everything in her world.

Her take on life changed dramatically following a profound experience revealing the connection between herself and the Universe - there's no separation. With this realisation, she no longer accepted the 'face-value' world she'd once thought of as the norm.

Renée Paule wishes to share this knowledge and show how a change of perspective can provide an alternative to the topsy-turvy world that Humanity, on the whole, accepts as an inevitable way of life.

She now lives in Ireland.

www.reneepaule.com

47591104R00075

Printed in Poland
by Amazon Fulfillment
Poland Sp. z o.o., Wrocław